Cooking Together

Having Fun with Two or More Cooks in the Kitchen

4880 Lower Valley Road   Atglen, Pennsylvania 19310

Other Schiffer Books By The Author:

Cooking Wild Game: 36 Hearty Dishes, 978-0-7643-3646-1, $19.99

Cooking with Mustard: Empowering your Palate, 978-0-7643-3643-0, $19.99

Other Schiffer Books on Related Subjects:

Today I Cook: A Man's Guide to the Kitchen, 978-0-7643-3644-7, $19.99

Creative Ideas for Garnishing & Decorating, 978-0-7643-3645-4, $19.99

Asparagus & Strawberries, 978-0-7643-3648-5, $19.99

Translated from the German by Dr. Edward Force
Recipes and Photos: G. Poggenpohl, Wismar
Food Styling: Caterina Poggenpohl
Layout and Typesetting: Sammler Kreativ GmbH

ISBN: 978-0-7643-3647-8
Printed in China

Schiffer Books are available at special discounts for bulk purchases for sales promotions or premiums. Special editions, including personalized covers, corporate imprints, and excerpts can be created in large quantities for special needs. For more information contact the publisher:

Published by Schiffer Publishing Ltd.
4880 Lower Valley Road
Atglen, PA 19310
Phone: (610) 593-1777; Fax: (610) 593-2002
E-mail: Info@schifferbooks.com

For the largest selection of fine reference books on this and related subjects, please visit our web site at
www.schifferbooks.com
We are always looking for people to write books on new and related subjects. If you have an idea for a book please contact us at the above address.

This book may be purchased from the publisher.
Include $5.00 for shipping.
Please try your bookstore first.
You may write for a free catalog.

In Europe, Schiffer books are distributed by
Bushwood Books
6 Marksbury Ave.
Kew Gardens
Surrey TW9 4JF England
Phone: 44 (0) 20 8392 8585; Fax: 44 (0) 20 8392 9876
E-mail: info@bushwoodbooks.co.uk
Website: www.bushwoodbooks.co.uk

G. Poggenpohl

Cooking Together

Having Fun with Two or More Cooks in the Kitchen

Contents

Foreword

Who likes to work alone in the kitchen? Cooking is a lot more fun when it's done by two! Partnership means sharing the work. Naturally, that also applies to cooking. Now, you might say, "I'll do the cooking and someone else can do the dishes!" But cooking together can make time in the kitchen a real joy.

For example, if you come home from work and haven't seen your spouse all day, there is usually much to talk about. And there's plenty of hunger, too. So, off you go to the kitchen to get busy together! With united efforts you will reach your goal much faster and happier, and you can talk while preparing and enjoying a delicious meal.

All the following recipes are planned so that everybody has practical tasks that fit together. You need only decide between yourselves who will be responsible for each step of the preparation, and then you can really cut loose. Perhaps you could open a bottle of wine or champagne first—that's a good first step in getting away from the day's work and finding relaxation.

You will see that cooking as a team is an effective way to leave the day's work behind you and enjoy a free evening. Or, get together with family or friends for a meal that begins with the joy of cooking together in the kitchen.

Yours,

G. Poggenpohl

Measurements

Both metric and standard equivalents are used in these recipes. As a reference, here is a list of abbreviations used for the metric quantities and some common metric conversions.

kg kilogram
g   gram
ml milliliter
1l   1 liter = 1000 ml = 1 kg = 1000 g

For Two People

Long day at work? Hungry as a wolf? A good friend is visiting? Then off to the supermarket, get the needed ingredients, and plunge into the joy of cooking together! Who wants to spend time in the kitchen alone when it's so much more fun together!

Prepare a meal together, and presto, it's on the table in no time and you have the perfect start to a lovely evening. No limits are set for sharing the tasks. For example, one participant can do prep work, such as cutting onions or peeling potatoes, and the other can stir the pot on the stove.

In the process you can talk a lot, swap stories and compare notes… or take up the challenge to a round of sudoku or hangman while the noodles are cooking. The fun is pre-programmed in every case.

Have Fun!

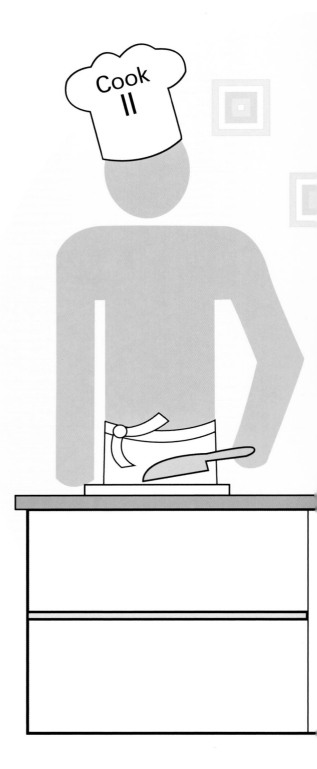

Skewered Sausages on Green Salad

Directions for Cook I

1. Wash the peppers, cut them in half, take out the seeds, and cut the peppers into slices 3/4 inch (2cm) thick. If possible, the strips should be just as long as the sausages.

2. Then stick the sausages on the skewer, alternating with the pepper strips.

3. Heat the frying fat in a pan on medium heat and fry both sides of the sausages until they are nice and brown.

Ingredients

12 bratwurst or other sausage
1/2 lb (200g) arugula
1 head of red lettuce
1 yellow pepper
1 red pepper
2 long wooden skewers
1 tablespoon frying fat
1 tablespoon olive oil
2 tablespoons wine vinegar
1 teaspoon sugar
salt
pepper
1 baguette
2 teaspoons of medium hot mustard

Hearty appetite!

Did you know ...

... that there are many legends about the origin of the bratwurst? One of them, for example, says that the diameter of the Nuremberg Bratwurst is small so that prisoners in the Nuremberg Prison could have their relatives and friends supply them with the slim sausages through the keyhole. As to whether there is any truth in this legend—well, it could be possible...

Directions for Cook II

1. Clean the arugula and cut out the hard stems. Then wash it and let it dry.

2. Also clean and wash the red lettuce, then cut it into bite-size chunks, divide between two bowls, and pour the dressing over it.

3. Finally, put a sausage on each salad and serve along with mustard and a piece of bread.

Pork Fillet with Roasted Chicory

Directions for Cook I

1. Grate the rind off of the lime, cut the lime in half, and squeeze out the juice. Put the juice and the lime aside.

2. Wash the pork fillet under cold running water and then pat dry. Then season it with salt and pepper.

3. Heat the frying fat in a pot and fry the fillet on all sides for 12 to 15 minutes, depending on thickness. Take the meat from the pot, wrap it in aluminum foil, and keep it warm. As soon as your partner is finished preparing the chicory, slice the pork into slices about 3/4 inch (2cm) thick.

4. Meanwhile, cook the pork drippings with three tablespoons of water, and then add the cream, the lime zest and juice, and salt and pepper to taste.

Ingredients

1 lb (500g) pork fillet
4 heads of chicory
1 untreated lime
1 tablespoon frying fat
3 tablespoons water
1 cup of fine cream
1 tablespoon butter
1 tablespoon sugar
3 tablespoons balsamic vinegar
aluminum foil
salt
pepper
white bread
herbs for garnish

Hearty appetite!

On your mark, get set, go!

Who wants to wash dishes right after a meal? Usually nobody volunteers. So, work it out with an old fashioned game of rock, paper, scissors. Sit or stand facing each other. Count to three, and on three each player uses a hand to form one of three possible symbols: rock, paper, or scissors. The scissors cut the paper, the rock dulls the scissors, and the paper wraps the stone. If both show the same form, simply try again. Play the best of three rounds to determine the winner, and who will be washing the dishes.

Directions for Cook II

1. Remove the outer leaves of the chicory, wash the rest, pat it dry and cut it in half. Select a few nice twigs of herbs for the garnish, wash, and shake dry.

2. Heat the butter in a pan, add the sugar, and stir until it melts. Put in the chicory halves, fry about three minutes, turn and brown briefly. Work carefully so the chicory does not fall apart! Finally, pour on the vinegar and season with salt and pepper.

3. Plate the cooked chicory, add the cut-up fillet, and serve along with the sauce, herbs, and white bread.

Rosemary Steak with Kohlrabi and Vegetables

Directions for Cook I

1. Wash the kohlrabi, peel it, cut into slices about 3/8 inch (1cm) thick, and then into strips.

2. Heat the butter in a pot, briefly steam the kohlrabi strips, pour in the water and cook covered about 10 minutes. Then stir in the fresh cream and season to taste with salt and pepper.

3. Wash the steaks under cold running water and pat them dry. Heat one tablespoon of oil in a pan and fry the steaks about five minutes. After turning them, add the rosemary twigs and fry another five minutes. Season the steaks with salt and pepper after frying.

Ingredients

2 beef steaks, about 1/2 lb (200g) each
2 kohlrabi
2-3 medium potatoes (2 1/4-3 1/4")
1 tablespoon butter
1/3 cup (70mL) water
1 cup fresh cream
2 tablespoons oil
2 stalks rosemary
salt
pepper
2 stalks parsley for garnish

Hearty appetite!

Caution, Think!

If one of you has a little spare time between tasks, you can work on a really hard puzzle: This spiral of matchsticks can be turned into three squares by moving only four matchsticks. Do you know how? (solution on page 78)

Directions for Cook II

1. Wash the potatoes, peel, and then cut into eighths.

2. Heat one tablespoon of oil in a pan, put in the potatoes and fry them. Turn them frequently until they are nice and brown. Season with salt and pepper.

3. Meanwhile, wash the parsley, shake it dry, and cut into small pieces. Sprinkle the parsley on the kohlrabi after dishing it out.

4. Place the finished steaks on plates with the kohlrabi and potato.

Chicken Liver with Cherry Tomatoes on Noodles

Directions for Cook I

1. Wash the liver under cold running water, pat it dry, and cut into bite-size pieces. Put the pieces into a bowl, mix with the cornstarch, vinegar, sugar, and star anise. Marinate about 20 minutes.

2. Meanwhile, wash the cherry tomatoes and cut the larger ones in half. Take a few nice twigs from the parsley stalk, wash, and shake dry.

3. Finally, divide everything on plates and garnish with parsley.

Ingredients

1/2 lb (250g) chicken liver
7 oz (200g) egg noodles
1 1/4 cups (200g) cherry tomatoes
1 teaspoon cornstarch
1 tablespoon balsamic vinegar
1 teaspoon brown sugar
2 star anise
1 tablespoons frying fat
salt
pepper
1 stalk parsley for garnish

Hearty appetite!

Did you know…

…that the longest noodle in the world was made on November 20, 2004, by Shenjli Chen, the chef of the Wang Fu Chinese restaurant in Vienna? As attested by a notary, he made a noodle 590 feet (180 meters) long out of a mass of dough weighing 3.3 lbs (1.5 kilograms). Until then the record was 182 feet (55.5 meters).

Directions for Cook II

1. Prepare the noodles according to the directions on the package.

2. Heat the fat in a pan, add your partner's marinated pieces of liver, and fry for about five minutes. Then pour the rest of the marinade over them, add some water if needed, and season to taste with salt and pepper. Mix the cherry tomatoes into the sauce only shortly before serving. They should just get hot.

3. When the cooking is done, shake the noodles, and let them dry well.

Rabbit with Balsamic Shallots

Directions for Cook I

1. Wash the rabbit under cold running water, pat it dry, remove the meat from the bones, and cut into cubes.

2. Wash the herbs and shake them dry. Cut the lemon in half and then in eighths. Peel the garlic cloves and chop them finely. Break off a few twigs of the sage stem for garnish, wash, and shake dry.

3. Heat one tablespoon of olive oil in a large pan and fry the pieces of meat until brown. Add the garlic, herbs, and lemon pieces and fry about three minutes. Season with salt and pepper. Remove the ingredients from the pan and keep warm.

4. Pour the rest of the oil into the pan and fry your partner's baguette slices until golden brown.

Ingredients

1/2 rabbit, about 2 3/4 lbs (1/3 kg)
1 1/4 cup (300g) shallots
1/2 bag mixed herbs
1 whole lemon
2 garlic cloves
3 tablespoons olive oil
1 baguette stick
1 tablespoon butter
1 tablespoon sugar
3 1/3 tablespoons (50ml) balsamic vinegar
salt
pepper
1 stalk sage for garnish

Hearty appetite!

Everybody Loves Sudoku

Meanwhile, will there be time for a little round of sudoku? The fascinating game from Japan has already taken the world by storm and will surely capture you too! The goal of the game is to fill in the grids using the numbers 1 through 9. However, no number can be repeated in a row, diagonally, or within any of the 9 squares. Very challenging—but absolutely enchanting! (solution on page 78)

	2					9		
	1	6	5	3	2			
8	3						5	1
	4			6			1	
	6		4	3	5		9	
	9			2			4	
3	2						6	8
		6	2	9	8	4		
		5				7		

Directions for Cook II

1. Peel the shallots and depending on their size either leave them whole or cut them in half. Slice the baguette and have the pieces ready for your partner.

2. Melt the butter in a pot, add the shallots, and fry briefly. Add the sugar and let them caramelize, then rinse with the vinegar (**NOTE**: don't put your head too close to the pot—the vinegar will rise unpleasantly to your nose!) and cook covered for about 10 minutes. Stir gently now and then. Then season to taste with salt and pepper.

3. Plate the rabbit meat along with the shallots. Garnish with the sage, dig in, and enjoy.

Paprika Meatballs with Rosemary Roasted Potatoes

Directions for Cook I

1. Wash the potatoes, peel them, and cut them into slices, cutting the larger ones in half first. Wash the rosemary stalks, shake dry, and pick the leaves from the stems.

2. Heat the oil in a pan, put the potato slices in and fry for about 10 minutes. Add the rosemary after 5 minutes, keep turning the potatoes, and season with salt and pepper.

3. Meanwhile, melt the butter in a pot and add the pepper strips from your partner. Now add water, cook covered for about 10 minutes, and season to taste with salt and pepper.

4. Pick a few nice leaves from the parsley stalks, wash, and shake dry.

Ingredients

1/2 lb (250g) ground beef
2-3 medium potatoes (2 1/4-3
1/4")
1 red pepper
1 yellow pepper
2 stalks rosemary
1 tablespoon oil
1 tablespoon butter
3 1/3 tablespoons (50ml) water
1 small onion
1 heaping tablespoon sweet
paprika powder
1 egg
1 tablespoon standard flour
salt
pepper
1 stalk parsley for garnish

Hearty appetite!

Direct Hit—Sunk!

On two sheets of graph paper, mark an x axis with coordinates from 1 to 11 and a y axis from A to K. Each player takes a sheet and marks off the following ships on their respective playing fields: one battleship (5 boxes), two destroyers (4 boxes), three cruisers (3 boxes), and four submarines (2 boxes). The ships may not touch each other. Players take turns firing on their opponent's ships by announcing an x and y coordinate. The player being fired on tells the opponent if he/she has struck a ship or not, and marks the shot on the playing field. A player who hits a ship can shoot again. The first player to sink all the enemy ships wins.

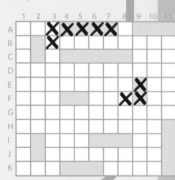

Directions for Cook II

1. Peel the onion and cut it finely. Wash the peppers and cut off their tops about 3/4 inch (2cm) down. Take out the stem and finely chop the pepper tops. Cut the rest of the peppers into strips and give them to your partner.

2. Put the ground meat into a bowl, add the paprika powder, egg, flour, onion, pepper tops, and mix well. Season to taste with salt and pepper. Form the meat into round balls about 2 inches (5cm) in diameter.

3. Heat some oil in a pan, put the meatballs in the hot oil, press them some what flat, and fry on both sides over moderate heat for about 12 minutes total.

4. Plate the meatballs, adding the potatoes and peppers. Garnish with the parsley and dig in.

Turkey Steaks with Prosecco Foam Sauce

Directions for Cook I

1. Prepare the noodles according to the instructions on the package.

2. While the noodles are cooking, wash the turkey steaks under cold running water, pat dry, and fry on both sides over moderate heat for about 10 minutes. Then season with salt and pepper.

3. Rinse the noodles in a colander and let them dry well.

4. Pick a few nice leaves from the basil stem for the garnish, wash, and shake dry.

Ingredients

2 1/2-lb (2000) turkey steaks
14 oz (400g) egg noodles
2/3 cup (150ml) prosecco
1 tablespoon frying fat
8 egg yolks
1 teaspoon mustard (medium hot)
sugar
salt
pepper
1 stalk basil for garnish

Hearty appetite!

Don't Get Hanged!

You certainly remember the Hangman game from your school days, but here's a refresher just in case! One player thinks of a long word (such as "skyscraper"), the other has to find it by asking for letters. When a guessed letter is not in the word, a body part is added on the gallows until the word is determined or the guesser is hung on the gallows.

Directions for Cook II

1. Half-fill a pot with water and heat it, but do not let it boil. Place a metal mixing bowl or a smaller pot in the water bath. **NOTE**: a double-boiler also works.

2. Put the egg yolk and mustard in the bowl and mix them with a whisk. Add the prosecco, stirring constantly, and beat the mixture thing until the sauce coagulates and becomes foamy. **NOTE**: It is very important to keep the water from boiling, otherwise the bowl will get too hot and the sauce will flake because of the egg yolk! Then take the bowl out of the water bath and season to taste with sugar, salt, and pepper.

3. Plate the turkey steaks with the noodles and pour the sauce over them. Garnish with the basil and serve.

Lamb Cutlets with Rice and Herbs

Directions for Cook I

1. Prepare the rice according to the directions on the package.

2. Meanwhile, wash the mixed herbs, shake dry, and cut them up. Take a few nice leaves from the basil stem for the garnish, wash, and shake dry.

3. Wash the lamb cutlets under cold running water and pat dry. Then fry the cutlets in hot frying fat for about five minutes with your partner's prepared garlic slices and rosemary stems. Add salt and pepper. Remove the rosemary and garlic before serving.

4. Heat olive oil in a pot, add the prepared rice, heat briefly, then fold in the herbs.

Ingredients

2 1/2-lb (200g) lamb cut-
lets
1 2/3 cups (300g) rice
1/2 bag mixed herbs
1 tablespoon frying fat
2 cloves garlic
2 stalks rosemary
2 tablespoons olive oil
1 tomato
2 zucchini
1 tablespoon butter
salt
pepper
1 stalk basil for garnish

Hearty appetite!

X Against O

Clearing the table—a dismal job, right? Simply avoid it with a win in Tic-tac-toe. One player uses X, the other O. You take turns writing your symbol in one of nine boxes. Whoever makes a row of three (horizontal, vertical, or diagonal) first wins the game.

Directions for Cook II

1. Wash the tomato, halve it, remove the seeds and cut the flesh into small cubes. Wash the zucchini, halve them lengthwise, and cut into strips. Peel the garlic cloves, cut one finely, and slice the other.

2. Heat the butter in a pot, fry the finely cut garlic, and add the zucchini strips. If the zucchini does not give off any liquid, add about two table spoons of water and steam covered for about seven minutes. Then stir in the tomato cubes and season the vegetables to taste with salt and pepper.

3. Put the lamb, rice, and vegetables on plate, garnish with basil, and serve.

Mediterranean Fried Potatoes

Directions for Cook I

The next time you want to make fried potatoes, try this unusual variety for a change. You can enjoy it as a standalone, but it tastes every bit as good along with fried meats such as thin beefsteak, lamb, or fried fish.

1. Wash the potatoes thoroughly, peel, halve and cut into finger-thick pieces.

2. Cut the olives into slices. Pick the arugula apart, wash, and remove thick stems. Take the anchovies out of the jar, let them drain, and have them ready.

Ingredients

2-3 medium potatoes (2
1/4-3 1/4")
1/4 lb (100g) pitted black
olives
1/2 lb (200g) arugula
6 anchovies
3 tablespoons oil
pepper

Hearty appetite!

Did you know…

… that the potato was long known as the "fruit of darkness"? The Europeans of the 16th and 17th centuries were not accustomed to eating food from out of the ground. They regarded this strange vegetable, brought to Europe from the Andes of South America by the Spanish Conquistadores, with fear and prejudice. After all, everything that comes from the ground might come from the devil!

Directions for Cook II

1. Heat the oil in a pan, add the potato pieces, and fry them until they are crisp. Now, add the olives and season to taste with pepper.

2. Just before serving, put the arugula and anchovies in the pan, mix them in, and immediately put everything on the plates.

Colorful Meat Skewers with Potato Pancakes

Directions for Cook I

1. Wash the peppers, zucchini, and eggplant. Halve the peppers, re move the seeds, and cut into bite-size chunks. Halve the zucchini and cut into slices. Cut the eggplant into bite-size cubes.

2. Wash the meat under cold running water and pat dry. Then cut the meat into cubes. Skewer the meat, followed by the pepper, zucchini, and eggplant, and then salt and pepper them. Put frying fat into a pan and fry the kebabs for about 10 to 15 minutes, turning them at times.

3. Meanwhile, wash the parsley, shake it dry, remove the green leaves from the stems, and chop it finely. Peel the shallot and cut finely. Then mix the parsley and shallots with the fresh cream.

ingredients

2/3 lb (300g) pork, about 1 1/8" thick
2-3 medium potatoes (2 1/4-3 1/4")
1 red and 1 yellow pepper
1 zucchini
1 small eggplant
4 long wooden skewers
1 tablespoon frying fat
2 stems parsley
1 shallot
1/4 cup (70g) fresh cream
3 1/3 tablespoons (50ml)
vegetable oil
salt
pepper
1 stalk basil for garnish

Hearty appetite!

Yes—No—Maybe?

Do you enjoy question-and-answer games? Here's a fun one! The first player asks the other various questions, such as "What is your name?" or "What are you wearing today?", etc. The person answering the question, however, can not answer with "Yes", "No", or "Maybe." So, in between asking question a player tries to fake out the answerer by asking him a question such as "Your jacket is blue, isn't it?" If a player gets caught responding with the forbidden answers, the other player wins. It's lots of fun, because somebody is guaranteed to fall into the trap!

Directions for Cook II

1. Wash the potatoes, peel then, and shred them into a sieve. It is best to put the sieve in a bowl so the water dripping from the potatoes doesn't make a mess.

2. Heat the oil in a pan and always put as many potato cakes into the pan as you can. They should have a diameter of about 3 inches (8cm) and a thickness of about 2/3 inch (1cm). While frying them, season them with salt and pepper, and turn them often. Take a few nice leaves from the basil stalk for garnish, wash them, and shake them dry.

3. Arrange the meat skewers on the plate with the potato cakes. Add the mixed fresh cream to the potato pancakes, garnish with the basil, and serve. A crisp slice of baguette will go very well with them.

Tip: Skewers are not only suitable for using up leftover vegetables, they can also be used to make tasty desserts using slices of plum, peach, or pineapple.

Tomatoes and Rice with Pork

Directions for Cook I

1. Peel the onion and chop it up finely. Wash the tomato and cut it into small cubes. Take a few nice leaves from the parsley stem, wash, and shake dry. Heat a tablespoon of oil in a large pot, cook the onion in it, add the rice, and fry briefly. Then stir the tomato paste into the rice and heat it. Now, add enough water to cover the rice.

2. The rice should be stirred often so the starch doesn't settle to the bottom and, in the worst case, burn. Let the rice cook for 20 minutes, occasionally checking the water level. If the rice absorbs all of the water in less than 20 minutes, add just enough water to cover the rice.

3. Stir in the tomato cubes shortly before serving and season to taste with salt.

Fully Logical!

Here we have a small puzzle for people who like to take a short break from cooking. Look carefully at the circles with the patterns. Which patterns must logically appear in the two circles in the lower right to complete the square properly? (solution on page 78)

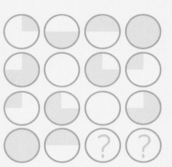

Directions for Cook II

1. Wash the meat under cold running water, pat dry, and cut into bite-size chunks.

2. Heat the frying fat in a pot, add the sugar, and melt it, stirring. Then add the meat and fry it until it's nice and brown all over. If the pieces of meat are not too thick, they will be done in 5 to 10 minutes. Then add the sour cream, stir, and season to taste with salt and pepper.

3. Arrange the tomato rice and meat on the plates, garnish with the parsley, and enjoy.

Cordon Bleu with Fried Potatoes and Lettuce

Directions for Cook I

1. Halve the ham and the cheese. Wash the pork cutlets under cold running water and pat dry. With a sharp knife, cut a pocket in the cutlets. Season the meat inside the pocket and all over with salt and pepper. Fill each pocket with half a slice of ham and cheese and close it with two toothpicks.

2. Roll the stuffed pork in the mixture of flour, egg, and breadcrumbs that your cooking partner prepared. Press the pork firmly in the mixture.

3. Heat the frying fat in a pan and fry the cordon bleu for about 5 minutes.

4. Meanwhile, make a salad dressing of the olive oil, vinegar, sugar, salt, and pepper. Pour the dressing over the lettuce your partner prepared and mix it all.

Ingredients

2 thick pork cutlets about 1/2 lb (200g) each
2-3 medium potatoes (2 1/4-3 1/4")
1 head oak leaf lettuce
1 slice cooked ham
1 slice full-flavored cheese (e.g. Gruyère)
4 toothpicks
2 tablespoon flour
1 egg
3 tablespoons breadcrumbs
1 tablespoon frying fat
1 tablespoon olive oil
2 tablespoon wine vinegar
2 tablespoon vegetable oil
sugar
salt
pepper
1 stalk of basil for garnish

Hearty appetite!

Cheeseboxes

This game is guaranteed to fascinate you! Simply take a piece of graph paper and two pencils. Whoever has the first turn may draw a line along the border of two squares. The goal of the game is to capture as many squares as possible by drawing the last "open" line and marking the square with an "X" or a circle. If you complete a square, you can draw another line. At the same time you have to think defensively and prevent the other player from closing a box. The winner has the most squares at the end of the game.

Directions for Cook II

1. Prepare three plates and fill one with flour, a beaten egg, and breadcrumbs.

2. Wash and peel the potatoes, halve them, and cut into slices. Wash the lettuce, separate the larger leaves, and let them drip dry. Take a few nice leaves from the basil stalk for the garnish, wash and, shake dry.

3. Heat the vegetable oil in a pan and fry the potato slices. Turn them carefully so they do not get mashed. After about 15 minutes, season with salt and pepper.

4. Arrange the cordon bleu with the fried potatoes, garnish with the basil, and add the lettuce.

Pork Cutlets with Mushroom Sauce

Directions for Cook I

1. Remove the dirt from the mushrooms with a brush and clean them. Halve the larger mushrooms or cut them into slices.

2. Heat the oil in a pot and fry the onions your partner has prepared. On high heat add the mushrooms. Then add water and cook for five to ten minutes.

3. Meanwhile stir some cold water into the cornstarch, then add it to the mushrooms, stirring. Cook the mixture and season with salt and pepper.

Ingredients

2 pork cutlets, about 1/2 lb
(200g) each
1 lb (500g) mushrooms in
season (champignon or others)
1 cup (200g) rice
1 tablespoon vegetable oil
1 small onion
1 teaspoon cornstarch
3 tablespoon flour
1 tablespoon frying fat
salt
pepper
1 stalk parsley for garnish

Hearty appetite!

Beware of Number Jugglers!

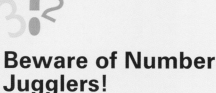

Need a little pastime for your spare moments? No problem! This number pyramid is quite a hard nut to crack—just right for inventive folks who don't give up easily. Identify the logic pattern in the puzzle and determine the number missing from the top of the pyramid. (solution on page 78)

?
10	8
5	6	3
2	4	3	1

Directions for Cook II

1. Prepare the rice as directed on the package. While the rice is cooking, peel the onion and cut into small cubes for your partner. Take a few nice leaves from the parsley stalk for the garnish, wash, and shake dry.

2. Wash the pork under cold running water and pat dry. Then season with salt and pepper and roll in the flour. Heat the frying fat in a pan and fry the cutlets on both sides for about five minutes.

3. Arrange the pork and the rice on plates and pour the mushroom sauce over them. Garnish with parsley and serve. **NOTE:** If you gather the mushrooms yourself, leave out any mushroom that gives you pause. It is best to take your "harvest" to an expert or grocer where they can be checked.

Fried Salmon on Chili Apples

Directions for Cook I

1. Squeeze the lemon. Cut the chili pepper in half lengthwise, remove the seeds, and cut into small cubes. Then wash your hands thoroughly, as the emerging chili juice is acidic.

2. Wash the apples, quarter them, remove the core, and cut into slices. Put the apple slices in a bowl, pour the lemon juice over them, and mix well.

3. Take a few nice leaves from the sage stalk for the garnish, wash, and shake dry.

```
ingredients

2 1/2-lb (200g) salmon
steaks
4 apples
1 lemon
1 small chili pepper
2 tablespoon butter
1 tablespoon sugar
salt
pepper
white bread
1 stalk sage for garnish

Hearty appetite!
```

Do You Know Kakuro?

A bonus for all sudoku fans, Kakuro, the exciting new number puzzle from Japan is here! The goal of this game is to fill in the empty squares in the grid system with numbers 1 to 9 so that the sum of each line equals the number in yellow at the end of each row or column. The numbers can only be used once per line. Caution, it is addictive! (solution on page 78)

Directions for Cook II

1. Wash the salmon steaks under cold running water and pat dry. Heat a tablespoon of butter in a pan and fry the two salmon steaks over low heat. Season with salt and pepper.

2. Heat the rest of the butter in a pot, stir in the sugar, and melt it. When the sugar is melted, add the apple slices and chili that your partner prepared. Cook briefly and stir. Season with a pinch of salt.
NOTE: Don't cook the apple slices too long, or they will become mushy!

3. Plate the fish, garnish with sage, and serve with white bread.

Duck Breast on Brussels Sprouts with Fried Baguette

Directions for Cook I

1. Wash the Brussels sprouts, cut the stems off, and remove the outer leaves. Cut the baguette into slices.

2. Heat the butter in a pot, add the Brussels sprouts, add water, and cook covered for about eight minutes. Then drain the pot, leaving the sprouts in, season with salt and pepper, and mix.

3. Gradually fry the baguette slices in the pan with the duck fat your partner has prepared.

Ingredients

1 duck breast, about 2/3 lb
(300g)
1 lb (500g) Brussels sprouts
2 baguettes
1 tablespoon butter
3 1/3 tablespoons (50ml)
water
1 teaspoon sweet paprika
powder
1 tablespoon frying fat
aluminum foil
salt
pepper

Hearty Appetite!

Well Hidden!

The Brussels sprouts are bubbling in the pot, do you have time for a short puzzle? Wonderful! Then we have just the right challenge for you: a picture puzzle that will make your head steam!

Can you recognize what object is hidden behind the boxes? Small hint: look around your kitchen…! (solution on page 79)

Directions for Cook II

1. Remove the pin feathers from the duck breast (singeing with a propane torch works best). Then wash the breast under cold running water, pat dry, and score the skin side with a sharp knife. Rub the paprika, salt, and pepper into the meat.

2. Heat the frying fat in a pan and fry the duck breast with the skin side down over high heat for about five minutes. Turn the meat over, fry another ten minutes at medium heat, then wrap it in aluminum foil and let it rest.

3. Finally, take the duck breast out of the foil, cut into slices and arrange with the Brussels sprouts and baguette slices.

Two Adults and Two Children

Has your daughter asked you for the third time when you'll finally have dinner ready? Is your youngest tugging on you impatiently? Then it is high time for some family cooking action! Depending on their age, you can transfer smaller or even larger tasks to your children. Most kids are excited when they can lend a hand in the kitchen.

Not only will your kids learn a lot about cooking, nutrition, and food, cooking together can be a fun family time as well. Especially when you play games like City-Country-River or I Pack My Suitcase while your meal cooks. You will see how much fun your children will have with this learning by doing method.

The following recipes are written so that the tasks are divided between two adults. Only you know best which tasks your junior chefs are ready for. Delegate tasks and challenges so your children can help throughout the meal prep.

Have Lots of Fun Together!

Chicken Wings with French Fries

Directions for Cook 1

1. Prepare a marinade for the chicken wings with two tablespoons of oil, two tablespoons of paprika powder, honey, tomato ketchup, salt, and pepper.

2. Wash the chicken wings under cold running water, pat dry, and brush on the marinade—a rather messy process that your children will love!

3. Then heat two tablespoons of oil in a large pan and fry the chicken wings until crisp, about 15 minutes.

Ingredients

1 3/4 lb (800) chicken wings
3-4 medium potatoes (2 1/4-3 1/4")
6 tablespoons oil
4 teaspoons sweet paprika powder
2 tablespoons honey
1 tablespoon tomato ketchup
parchment paper
salt
pepper
1 stalk parsley for garnish
1 bottle tomato ketchup

Hearty appetite!

Off to the Picnic!

The chicken wings are marinated and are crackling in the pan. Time for a little game, isn't it? One person starts with: "I pack my picnic basket and put in [say a food or utensil]." The next player must repeat the complete sentence and add another object to it. Thus the chain gets longer and longer. Whoever cannot put all the objects together is eliminated.

Directions for Cook II

1. Make a sauce for the potatoes with two tablespoons of oil, two tablespoons of paprika powder, salt, and pepper. Stir the sauce.

2. Wash and peel the potatoes, halve them, and then cut them into strips. Line a baking pan with parchment paper, lay the potato strips on it and apply the sauce to them. Bake for about 15 minutes at 400°F (200°C).

3. Meanwhile, pick a few nice leaves from the parsley stalk for the garnish, wash, and shake dry. Arrange the chicken wings and the potato fingers on plates, garnish with the parsley, and serve with ketchup.

Tip: If you have a convection oven, you can bake the chicken wings and the potatoes simultaneously on two separate sheets.

Meatballs in Spiced Tomato Sauce

Directions for Cook I

1. Wash the tomatoes and cut the tops off with a sharp knife. Wash the herbs, shake dry, and cut up coarsely.

2. Bring water to a boil and briefly drop the tomatoes individually into the boiling water. When the skin starts to curl, take the tomatoes out, peal them, cut out the stem areas, and cut the pulp into small pieces.

3. Put the tomato paste into a pot, add the tomato pieces, and cook them. Let the sauce cook for about eight minutes, then add the herbs and season to taste with salt and pepper.

Ingredients

1 1/3 lb (600g) ground beef
10 tomatoes
1 package of mixed herbs
3 tablespoons tomato paste
1 onion
2 eggs
4 heaping tablespoons breadcrumbs
2 tablespoons oil
salt
pepper
1 cup (125g) shredded mozzarella cheese
1 baguette

Hearty appetite!

Have You Droodled?

In just a few minutes the meatballs will be ready. There is still time for two "droodles," which are small pictorial puzzles. In the below pictures, you are looking at small segments of a bigger picture. You must guess what the bigger picture is. Sometimes there are several solutions. So, go to it: what is this?
(solution on page 79)

Directions for Cook II

1. Peel the onion and cut it into fine cubes. Put the ground beef into a bowl, add the eggs, flour, breadcrumbs, and onion. Season the meat to taste with salt and pepper and mix everything well. Form meatballs about 1 1/2 inches (4cm) in diameter—children particularly enjoy this!

2. Heat the oil in a pan, put the meatballs in, flatten them somewhat, and fry them for five to six minutes on each side.

3. Plate the meatballs in the tomato sauce, sprinkle with the grated cheese, and serve with the sliced baguette.

Noodles with Tomato Meatball Sauce

Directions for Cook I

1. Peel the onions and dice them. Put the ground meat in a bowl, add the onion, and mix everything well by hand. Whether cookie dough or ground meat, kneading is fun for children! Season the mixture to taste with salt and pepper.

2. Heat a tablespoon of oil in a pot and cook the meat and onion mixture. Stir it frequently with a cooking spoon so that the meat remains crumbly. When the meat has browned, add the tomato paste, and cook it briefly. Then add the strained tomatoes and cook for about 15 minutes.

3. Finally, season to taste with some sugar, salt, and pepper.

Ingredients

1 lb (500g) noodles
1 lb (400g) ground meat
1 1/2 cups (400g) strained tomatoes
2 onions
3 tablespoons oil
3 tablespoons tomato paste
sugar
salt
pepper
1 cup (125g) shredded mozzarella cheese
1 stalk basil for garnish

Hearty appetite!

Those That Seek Shall Find...

Cooking is done just as diligently in this picture as it is in your house. But wait a moment—something is wrong… There are five details that differ between the two pictures. Each cook must find the five differences in the picture on the right. Keep track of everyone's time. Who was the fastest? (solution on page 79)

Directions for Cook II

1. Prepare the noodles as instructed on the package. Meanwhile, take a few nice basil leaves from the stalk for the garnish, wash, and shake dry.

2. When the noodles are cooked, strain them and let them dry in a colander.

3. Plate the noodles and cover with the tomato sauce. Sprinkle on the cheese and garnish with basil. Have a taste—you'll like it!

Creamed Pork with Pineapple Rice

Directions for Cook I

1. Prepare the rice as instructed on the package.

2. Meanwhile, peel the pineapple slices and cut into small cubes.

3. Melt the butter in a pot, heat the prepared rice in it, and add the pine apple pieces.

Tip: Cut the remaining pineapple into pieces and serve it as a side dish or as dessert.

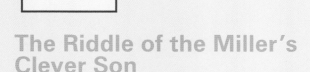

Ingredients

3 1/2-lb (200g) pork cut-
lets
2 cups (400g) rice
4 slices fresh pineapple, about
3/4 inch (2cm) thick
1 tablespoon butter
1 onion
1 tablespoon oil
1 cup sweet cream
1 teaspoon mustard seed
1 cup fresh cream
salt
pepper
1 stalk parsley for gar-
nish

Hearty appetite!

The Riddle of the Miller's Clever Son

Once upon a time there was a king who let himself play a gruesome joke on those condemned to death. They were allowed to make one statement. If it was true, they were beheaded—if it was false, they were hanged.

One day a miller's son was condemned to death and made his statement. The king was stunned—he could neither have him beheaded nor hanged! Do you know what the miller's son said? (solution on page 79)

Directions for Cook II

1. Peel the onion and dice it. Take a few leaves from the parsley stalk, wash, and shake dry.

2. Wash the pork under cold running water, pat dry, and cut into strips with a sharp knife.

3. Heat the oil in a pot, fry the onion, add the strips of pork, and cook for about ten minutes. Add the cream and mustard, reduce the heat, and let it cook for about 15 minutes. Then stir in the fresh cream and season to taste with salt and pepper.

4. Serve the pineapple rice with the creamed pork and garnish with the parsley.

Salami and Mozzarella Pizza

Directions for Cook I

1. Sift the flour into a bowl and mix in the salt. Crumble the yeast into lukewarm water, add the sugar, stir it in, and let it dissolve. Let the yeast stand for about ten minutes. Mix the yeast mixture with the flour and work in the oil until it has become a soft, smooth dough.

2. Let the dough stand covered for about 40 minutes in a warm place. Then knead it strongly and separate the dough into two balls. Roll the dough out into two round pizza crusts and place them on a baking sheet lined with parchment paper. NOTE: There are numerous operations that young folks can handle in this recipe. In particular, children always like to help make the dough.

3. Along with your partner, cover the pizza crusts with the tomato mixture they have prepared, as well as the salami and other toppings. Then sprinkle olive oil on the pizzas and bake them for 35 minutes, one after the other, in an oven preheated to 400°F (200°C). Then garnish the pizza with the basil and serve.

Ingredients

For the dough:
2 3/4 cups (350g) flour
1 1/2 cakes fresh yeast (25g)
or
1 1/2 active dry yeast packets
1 cup (250mL) lukewarm water
2 tablespoons olive oil
1 pinch of sugar
1 teaspoon salt
parchment paper

For the toppings:
2 onions
1 clove garlic
2 tomatoes
2 cups (250g) mozzarella
3/8 cup (100mL) strained tomatoes
2 tablespoons mixed herbs
1/4 lb (100g) salami
olive oil
salt, pepper
2 stalks basil for garnish

Hearty appetite!

City-Country-River (but with food)

The pizza is in the oven—that means half an hour before you and your family can eat. Just the right amount of time for a few rounds of city-country-river, perhaps with a change to beverage-fruit-vegetable-herb. Okay, to get started choose any letter. The first person to think of an answer for each category that begins with the chosen letter is the winner.

Example
Beverage: Apple juice
Fruit: Asian pear
Vegetable: Arugula
Herb: Anise

Directions for Cook II

1. Peel the onions, halve, and cut into strips. Peel the garlic clove and dice. Wash the tomatoes, halve, remove the core, and cube. Cut the mozzarella into strips.

2. Take a few leaves from the basil stalk for the garnish, wash, and shake dry. Pour the strained tomatoes into a bowl, stir in the garlic and herbs, and season to taste with salt and pepper.

Tip: If you have a convection oven, you can bake the pizzas simultaneously on two separate sheets at 350°F (180°C).

Warm Apple Pockets with Vanilla Sauce

Directions for Cook I

1. Squeeze the lemon and mix the juice with the sugar in a bowl. Break the egg, separate it, and put the yolk in a bowl.

2. Take a few leaves of the lemon mint for the garnish, wash, and shake dry.

3. Line a baking sheet with parchment paper. Place you partner's finished apple pockets on the sheet and brush with the egg yolk. Bake them in the oven for about 20 minutes at 350°F (180°C).

Ingredients

16 oz (450g) frozen puff pastry
4 apples
1 lemon
1 tablespoon sugar
1 egg
parchment paper
1 cup (200ml) vanilla sauce
1 stalk lemon mint for garnish

The Riddle Story of Romeo and Juliet

A riddle story describes an unusual situation, the account of which must be guessed. One reads the story aloud and asks the others what has happened. To find the answer, the others must ask the storyteller questions, such as "Did Romeo and Juliet die because they opened the window?" The storyteller may only answer their questions with "Yes, "No," or "That is not important." That makes everything more exciting!

And now go to it: Romeo and Juliet are lying dead on the floor, the window is open, there is a puddle of water on the floor—what has happened here? (solution on page 79)

Directions for Cook II

1. Wash the apples, quarter, and remove the cores. Cut into small pieces and mix with the lemon juice sugar mixture that your partner prepared.

2. Place a puff pastry on the baking pan, spoon out one or two table spoons of the apple pieces in the center. Fold the other puff pastry around it and press the open sides firmly together with a fork. Repeat this process for all of the pockets. Children can help wonderfully here in both filling and pressing!

3. After baking, plate the apple pockets and add the vanilla sauce. Garnish with the lemon mint and dig in.

Tip: The apple pockets taste good cold or hot. The same is true of the vanilla sauce. The dish tastes especially good if you use the two parts as opposites, i.e. a warm pocket with a cold sauce.

Milk Rice Pudding with Peaches

MAMA

Directions for Cook I

1. Heat 4 1/4 cups of milk in a pot, add the milk rice, and cook, stirring constantly—the children can stir it under your direction. Add the rest of the milk as soon as the rice has absorbed what was there. Repeat this for about 15 to 20 minutes until the rice is ready to eat. The end product will be a rice pudding that is not too firm.

2. Pour the flavored milk rice into a baking pan. Set the peaches that your partner prepared on the rice and bake in the oven for about 15 minutes at 350°F (180°C).

Tip: For this recipe, be sure to use milk rice, which can be bought as such at a specialty store with foods imported from northern Europe. Normal rice will not give the desired results.

Ingredients

500 grams milk rice
8 1/2 cups milk
1 whole lemon
2 tablespoons sugar
1 packet vanilla sugar
for flavoring
6 peaches

Hearty appetite!

I see something that you don't see, and it is…

Your children have been a big help. Are they getting bored now? No problem—keep them in the mood with the "I see something that you don't see" game until the meal is finished. For example, someone begins with "I see something that you don't see, and it is red!" Then the guessing begins:

"Is it the apple in the fruit bowl? Or dad's red T-shirt?"

"No, it is the ketchup bottle!"

Whoever solves the puzzle can start the next round. And soon the wait is over.

PAPA

Directions for Cook II

1. Use a microplane on the lemon and add the zest to the milk rice while your partner stirs it. Pour the sugar in and flavor with vanilla sugar.

2. Wash the peaches, halve them, remove the pits, cut into slices, and have them ready for your partner.

3. Once ready, cut the pudding into portions and plate them for service.

When Guests Come...

Invite your friends to a cooking party. For small groups it is a gigantic joy! Organize your guests into teams that compete against each other. A friendly competition between men and women is always lots of fun!

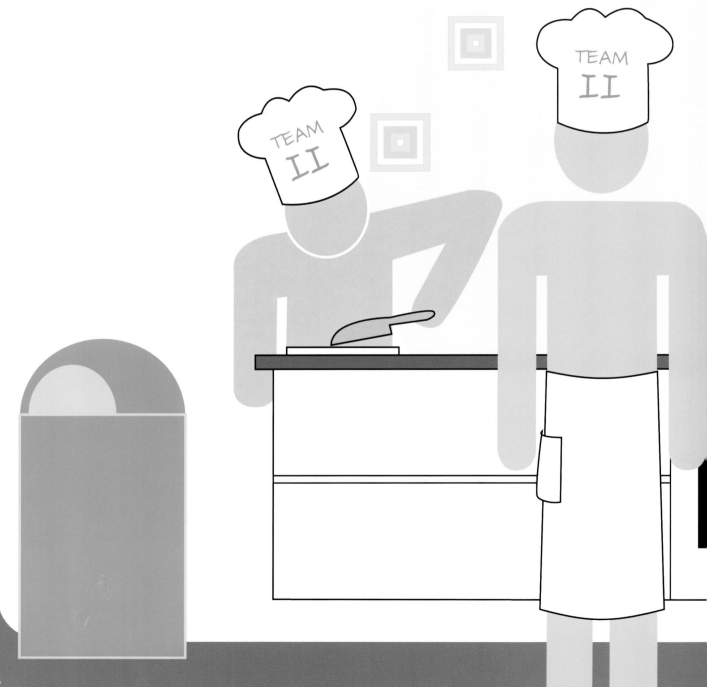

With the help of a party game such as Bottle-Fish or Snatch Up the Cherry, you decide which team must cut up the onions or garlic! Let your imagination run free and you will keep coming up with entertaining ideas that will make it loads of fun for everybody!

The recipes in this chapter are laid out for four people but can naturally be divided up for a larger number of guests.

Then off you go to enjoyment!

Minute Steaks with Herb Crust and Baked Potatoes

TEAM I

Directions for Team I

1. Wash the potatoes thoroughly and halve them lengthwise. Line a baking sheet with parchment paper and sprinkle the teaspoon of salt and the marjoram over it evenly.

2. Place the potato halves on the parchment paper with the cut sides down and bake in the oven for about 20 minutes at 350°F (180°C).

3. Meanwhile, wash and quarter the tomatoes. Take a few nice leaves from the basil for the garnish, wash, and shake dry.

Ingredients

4 thin 1/3-lb (150g) pork steaks
4-5 medium potatoes (2 1/4-3 1/4")
parchment paper
1 teaspoon salt
1 tablespoon dried marjoram
1 packet mixed herbs
1 tablespoon vegetable oil
1 cup (100g) grated swiss cheese
1 tablespoon frying fat
salt
pepper
1 tomato
1 stalk basil for garnish

Hearty appetite!

Bottle-Fish

Bottle-Fish is a party game that is guaranteed to put your guests in a good mood! Players count out loud one at a time, the first player starts with one. For every number that is divisible by five or has a five in it, the person whose turn it is must say "bottle." For every number that is divisible by seven or has a seven in it, the player must say "fish." Every time one of the two words is spoken, the direction of play reverses. The game ends at 35, when the player must say "Bottle-Fish." Caution: make one mistake and you are out!

TEAM II

Directions for Team II

1. Wash the mixed herbs, shake dry, and cut small. Then put them in a bowl and mix with the vegetable oil and cheese.

2. Wash the pork steaks under cold running water, pat dry, and season with salt and pepper. Heat the frying fat in a pan and fry the steaks on both sides.

3. Place the steaks in a baking pan, spoon the herb-cheese mixture on the steaks, and broil or grill them for five minutes, until the cheese is melted.

4. Plate the steaks with the potatoes and garnish with the tomato quarters and basil leaves.

Glazed Chicken Thighs on Italian Vegetables

Directions for Team I

1. Wash the chicken under cold running water and pat dry.

2. Put the chicken thighs on a baking sheet or in a large baking pan and brush them with the marinade that Team II made. Bake in a preheated oven at 350°F (180°C) for about 30 minutes.

3. Heat the oil in a wide pot or pan. Put the zucchini slices, eggplant pieces, and lemon eighths prepared by Team II in the hot oil and stew them. When the vegetables are finished, add the tomato pieces, and season with salt and pepper.

ingredients

4 chicken thighs
2 zucchinis
1 eggplant
2 tomatoes
1 whole lemon
1 tablespoon oil
1 tablespoon olive oil
1 tablespoon sugar beet syrup
1 tablespoon tomato paste
1 teaspoon rose paprika powder
salt
pepper
2 stalks basil for garnish

Hearty appetite!

Syl-la-ble-chain

Word games are always very popular at parties—probably because you don't need anything other than your brain to play. How about a syllable puzzle, for instance? The first player says a word (for example, "swordfish"). The next player must find a word that begins with the last syllable of the previous word, such as "fishtail." Then the third player would say a word starting with "tail," such as "tailwind." Whoever cannot continue the chain drops out.

TEAM II

Directions for Team II

1. Mix a brushable marinade using the olive oil, beet syrup, tomato paste, and paprika powder. Season with salt and pepper.

2. Wash the zucchini, eggplant, tomatoes, and lemon. Halve the zucchini and cut into slices, cut the eggplant into batonnet, and the lemon into eighths. Halve the tomatoes, remove the seeds, and cut them up. Have everything ready for Team I.

3. Take a few leaves from the basil stalks for the garnish, wash, and shake dry.

4. Place the chicken and vegetables on plates, garnish with the basil, and serve.

Pork Fillets with Stewed Cucumbers

TEAM I

Directions for Team I

1. Wash the pork fillets under cold running water, pat dry, and season with salt and pepper.

2. Heat the frying fat in a pan and fry the fillets on all sides, about 12 to 15 minutes depending on thickness. Take the meat out of the pan and wrap in aluminum foil.

3. Add water to the pork drippings, stir in the red currant jam, and season to taste with vinegar, salt, and pepper.

Ingredients

2 1-lb (400g) pork fillets
6-7 cucumbers (6 3/8"
long)
1 tablespoon frying fat
aluminum foil
3 1/3 tablespoons (50ml)
water
3 tablespoons red cur-
rant jam
3 tablespoons balsamic
vinegar
1 onion
1 tablespoon butter
salt
pepper
2 stalks basil for garnish

Hearty appetite!

Well Combined is Half Won!

Offer your friends this puzzle—some of them will really gnash their teeth. Of 100 members from a tennis club, 60 are women, 80 are married, 70 wear white sneakers, and 90 wear white socks. What is the lowest number of married women who wear white sneakers and socks? (solution on page 79)

TEAM II

Directions for Team II

1. Peel the onion and dice. Wash and peel the cucumbers, remove the seeds with a knife, and cut into pieces. Take a few leaves from the basil stalks for the garnish, wash, and shake dry.

2. Heat the butter in a pot, fry the onion pieces in it, add the cucumber pieces, and cook covered for about ten minutes. Season with salt and pepper.

3. Plate the cucumbers topped with the pork and currant jam sauce. Garnish with basil and enjoy the flavor.

Tip: Crisp Italian bread goes very well with this dish.

Leek Quiche

TEAM I

Directions for Team I

1. Sift the flour into a bowl and mix with a teaspoon of salt. Crumble the yeast into one cup of lukewarm water, add the sugar, and dissolve, stirring. Let it stand for ten minutes.

2. Mix the yeast mixture with the flour and work in the oil until a soft, smooth dough is formed. Let the dough rise covered in a warm place for about 40 minutes, then knead it strongly.

3. Roll out the dough and place it in a quiche or spring form, making a high edge. Add the leek strips Team II prepared and sprinkle on the pork cubes. Pour Team II's cream mixture on top of that and sprinkle the cheese on top. Bake in the oven for about 40 minutes at 350°F (180°C).

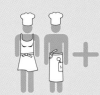

Ingredients

2 3/4 cups (350g) flour
1 teaspoon salt
1 1/2 cakes fresh yeast (25g) or
1 1/2 active dry yeast packets
1 pinch sugar
1 tablespoon olive oil
2 leeks
1/2 lb (250g) cubed pork
1 cup sweet cream
1 egg
2 cups (200g) shredded cheese
nutmeg
salt
pepper

Did you know...

...that the leek was very popular in ancient times? For example, the Roman emperor Nero was also known as Porrophagus (leek eater) because of his fondness for the vegetable. And the British king Cadwallader is said to have used the leek as a symbol for his Welsh troops around 640 B.C. To this day the leek is part of the Welsh coat of arms.

TEAM II

Directions for Team II

1. Cut the roots off the leeks and remove the outer skin. Then halve them and wash them thoroughly under running water. Let the leek halves dry well and cut them diagonally into strips.

2. Pour the cream into a bowl and add the egg to it. Mix everything well with a whisk. Season the mixture well with nutmeg, salt, and pepper so that it is ready for Team I.

3. Cut portions from the quiche and serve.

Meatballs on Leeks

Directions for Team I

1. Wash the sage stalks and shake them dry. Cut one of them finely and take a few leaves from the other for garnish. Peel the onions and dice.

2. Cut the roots off the leeks and remove the outer skin. Then halve them and wash them thoroughly under running water. Let the leek halves drip dry and cut them diagonally into strips.

3. Melt the butter in a pot, add the leek strips, and cook them. If the leeks do not give off enough liquid, add about 3 1/3 tablespoons (50ml) water. Cook them about seven minutes and then season with nutmeg, salt, and pepper.

Ingredients

1 1/2 lbs (700g) ground
meat
3 leeks
2 stalks sage (one for garnish)
2 onions
1 tablespoon butter
2 eggs
4 tablespoons breadcrumbs
3 tablespoons oil
nutmeg
salt
pepper

Hearty appetite!

Wandering is the Spoon's Joy

Should your guests get to know each other better? Then get out your spoons and go wandering. Tie a long string on each of two spoons and form two teams facing each other in rows. Each team member tries to slide its spoon through its clothing as quickly as possible from top to bottom. When the spoon reaches the last member of the team, reverse the order take the spoon through again. It doesn't matter who wins—the game is intended as an icebreaker and should create a relaxed mood.

TEAM
II

Directions for Team II

1. In a bowl, mix the ground meat with the eggs, Team I's onions, the breadcrumbs, and the cut-up sage. Season with salt and pepper. Then make meatballs out of the mixture.

2. Heat the oil in a pan and fry the meatballs on both sides over moderate heat for about 15 to 20 minutes, depending on their thickness.

3. Place the meatballs and leeks on plates, garnish with the sage, and enjoy the flavor.

Baked Turkey Cutlets with Mozzarella

Directions for Team I

1. Wash the turkey cutlets under cold running water and pat dry.

2. Heat the frying fat in a pan and fry the turkey cutlets on both sides. Meanwhile, season them with salt and pepper.

3. Take a few parsley leaves and spring onion shoots for the garnish, wash, and shake dry.

Ingredients

4 1/2-lb (200g) turkey cutlets
7 oz (200g) mozzarella
1 tablespoon frying fat
2 large tomatoes
8 anchovies
salt
pepper
1 baguette
1 stalk parsley and 1
spring onion for garnish

Hearty appetite!

The Riddle Story of Poor Charlie

Riddle stories are best suited for gatherings, where guessing the conclusion to an absurd story is much easier and more entertaining. The leader reads the story aloud and then asks what happened. The players must ask questions until they get the story straight. But don't forget—the story teller may only answer questions with "Yes," "No," or "That is not important." Otherwise he/she will reveal too much and end the game. That would not be fun. So here is the story:

Poor Charlie died when the man stopped talking. What happened? (solution on page 79)

TEAM II

Directions for Team II

1. Wash the tomatoes and cut into slices. Let the mozzarella drip dry and cut it into slices.

2. Prepare a baking pan, put in the fried cutlets from Team I, put two anchovies and two tomato slices on each one, and cover everything with mozzarella slices. Bake in the oven for about five minutes at 350°F (180°C).

3. Plate the cutlets, garnish with parsley and spring onions, and add slices of bread.

Asian Vegetable Dish

TEAM
I

Directions for Team I

1. Prepare the rice noodles and mushrooms as directed on the packages.

2. Meanwhile, wash the sugar peas and let them drip dry.

3. After cooking, shake the rice noodles and mushrooms and let them drip dry.

Ingredients

14 oz (400g) rice noodles
1 3/4 oz (50g) dried chinese mixed mushrooms
1 red and 1 yellow pepper
1 kohlrabi
1 jar of mung bean sprouts
4 carrots
1/4 cup (50g) ginger
8 tablespoons vegetable oil
1/2 lb (200g) sugar peas
2 tablespoons soy sauce
salt
pepper

Hearty appetite!

Eating with Chopsticks is Child's Play!

Put one stick in your right hand so that it lies back between your thumb and index finger. It is supported by the ring finger so that it does not move while eating. The second stick should be mobile and is placed between the index and middle fingers. If you bend the index and middle fingers slightly, you can hold the food with the tips of the sticks.

TEAM II

Directions for Team II

1. Wash the peppers, halve them, remove the seeds, and cut into strips. Wash and peel the kohlrabi and cut it into fine strips. Drain the bean sprouts. Wash the carrots, peel them, and cut into slices. Peel the ginger and dice.

2. Heat the oil in a pan or wok, add Team I's mushrooms, the ginger, carrot slices, kohlrabi, and pepper strips. Fry for about five minutes. Then mix in Team I's sugar peas. Finally, season the vegetables with soy sauce, salt, and pepper.

3. Plate the noodles, add the vegetables, and serve.

Marinated Beef Strips with Chinese Mushrooms

TEAM
I

Directions for Team I

1. Prepare the noodles and mushrooms as instructed on the packages.

2. Meanwhile, wash and clean the spring onions, then cut them into 3/4-inch (2cm) pieces. Shake the finished noodles and mushrooms and let them drip dry.

3. Melt the butter in a pot, briefly fry the noodles, and serve with the meat.

Ingredients

1 lb (400g) thin beefsteak
14 oz (400g) Asian egg noodles
1 3/4 oz (50g) dried chinese mixed mushrooms
2 bunches of spring onions
1 tablespoon butter
1 tablespoon olive oil
1 tablespoon honey
1 tablespoon soy sauce
1 tablespoon cornstarch
chinese chili sauce
1/2 cup (100ml) water
salt
pepper

Hearty appetite!

Everybody Can Draw!

In this game your guests must show creativity! Divide your guests into two groups and give each group paper and pencils or pens. Write ten challenging subjects on pieces of folded paper. Show the first subject to the first player from each team. Starting at the same time, the players must draw clues that help the team guess what the subject is. The artists are not permitted to speak. The group that identifies the subject first gets a point.

Second round: Now the second player of each group draws, and so on. The group that has the most points at the end wins.

TEAM II

Directions for Team II

1. Wash the beef under cold running water and pat it dry. Cut it in half lengthwise and then into strips about 3/4 inch (1cm) wide.

2. Make a marinade of the oil, honey, soy sauce, cornstarch, chili powder, salt, and pepper. Pour it over the beef strips, stir, and let sit for about an hour.

3. Take the meat out of the marinade. Heat a pan or wok, put the meat in and fry it until it is done. Then add Team I's spring onions and mushrooms. Add the marinade, pour water over it, and let it thicken into a sauce. Season with salt and pepper.

Garlic Herb Spaghetti

TEAM I

Directions for Team I

1. Wash the herbs, shake dry, and cut them coarsely. Peel and dice the garlic cloves.

2. Use a blender to make a pesto with the herbs, garlic, olive oil, and some salt.

3. Take a few nice leaves of the basil for the garnish, wash, and shake dry.

ingredients

16 oz (500g) spaghetti
1 bunch mixed herbs
4 garlic cloves
3 1/3 tablespoons (50ml)
olive oil
salt
pepper
2 stalks basil for garnish

Hearty appetite!

Snatch Up the Cherry!

Tie bunches of goodies on a long string (i.e. cherries, sausages, candies, etc.). Two people hold the string at about eye level, swinging it gently back and forth. One at a time, players must grab these items with their mouths, but they must keep their hands behind their backs. It's lots of fun watching people bob around for a morsel.

TEAM II

Directions for Team II

1. Prepare the spaghetti as directed on the package, strain it, and let it dry.

2. Plate the spaghetti and spread Team I's pesto over it. Then garnish with basil and serve.

Steamed Flounder on Bacon and Beans

Directions for Team I

1. Wash and clean the beans, cut off the tips, and pull the string off with a knife. Then halve the beans.

2. Wash the lemon in hot water, zest with a microplane and have it ready for Team II. Squeeze the lemon and keep the juice. Melt the butter in a wide pot and fry Team II's onion. Then add the cubed bacon and fry until done.

3. Then put the beans in the pot, pour in water, and season with salt and pepper. Cook the beans covered for about 15 minutes. After about ten minutes put the fish fillet that Team II prepared on the beans and steam them.

ingredients

1 3/4 lb (800g) flounder fillet
1 3/4 lb (800g) green beans
1/4 lb (100g) bacon
1 whole lemon
1 tablespoon butter
1 onion
1/3 cup (70ml) water
3/4 cup (200g) fresh cream
salt
pepper

Hearty appetite!

Crooked Compound Nouns

Want a word game for clever minds? Here it is: Every player writes the letters A to Z on a sheet of paper. Then a letter is chosen, for example C. Now the players have ten minutes to think of a compound noun beginning with each letter from A to Z, in which the second half of the word begins with C. No component may be used more than once. And whoever gets the most words wins.

Example:
Apple Cart
Baseball Cap
Clown Car
Dog Catcher
Egg Carton
Flute Case
Gerbil Cage

Directions for Team II

1. Peel the onion and dice. Cut the bacon into small cubes.

2. Wash the fish fillets under cold running water, pat dry, salt, and sprinkle with the Team I's lemon juice.

3. Carefully lift the finished fish fillet off the beans. Then stir the fresh cream into the beans and add the lemon zest that Team I prepared.

4. Plate the beans and place the fish on top.

Salmon with Noodles and Lemon Sauce

TEAM
I

Directions for Team I

1. Wash the salmon steaks under cold running water and pat dry.

2. Heat the oil in a pan and fry the salmon steaks on both sides for about ten minutes total.

3. Heat the butter in a pot, shake the flour over it, and heat briefly. Pour it all into the chicken broth, stirring. Cook the sauce, let it stand for 15 minutes, then add Team II's lemon zest and season with the lemon juice, salt, and pepper.

Ingredients

2 1/2-lb (200g) salmon steaks
17 1/2 oz (500g) egg noodles
1 whole lemon
1 tablespoon oil
2 tablespoons butter
3 tablespoons flour
1 cup (250ml) chicken broth
salt
pepper
2 stalks basil for garnish

Hearty appetite!

The Riddle Story of the Three Shipwrecked Sailors

Hear is another riddle story that will drive your guests to despair. Three shipwrecked sailors land on a lonely island without food. They decide that one of them must die so the other two may live long enough to be rescued. After only five seconds they reach a decision regarding who the unlucky one should be. What has happened? (solution on page 79)

TEAM II

Directions for Team II

1. Wash the lemon in hot water and zest with a microplane. Squeeze the lemon and have the juice ready for Team I. Take a few leaves from the basil stalks for garnish, wash, and shake dry.

2. Prepare the noodles as instructed on the package. Cut Team I's fried salmon into small pieces. Remove any bones, and add the fish to the sauce.

3. When the noodles are cooked, strain, and plate them. Pour the sauce over them and garnish with basil. Enjoy your meal!

Tip: You can add fresh Italian bread.

Solutions

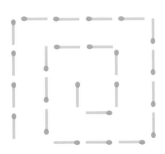

Page 13

Page 17

6	5	2	1	8	4	9	7	3
9	7	1	6	5	3	2	8	4
8	3	4	9	7	2	6	5	1
2	4	3	8	6	9	5	1	7
1	6	7	4	3	5	8	9	2
5	9	8	7	2	1	3	4	6
3	2	9	5	4	7	1	6	8
7	1	6	2	9	8	4	3	5
4	8	5	3	1	6	7	2	9

Page 29

Here's how you find the right circles: Divide the square into four small squares. Begin in the upper left corner and repeat the pattern of the first square in the other three. Now rotate the four squares counterclockwise 90 degrees and switch the colors.

Page 33

The right number is 17. The value of every box is the sum of the two under it minus 1.

Page 35

		1	3				7	1
	5	4	2		7	9	8	5
5	3	2	1		6	7	9	3
8	4		6	9	8		5	2
7	1		4	7	9	8		
9	2	1				9	6	8
	3	2	1	5		5	1	
3	9		8	7	6		8	4
2	7	1	4		8	6	9	7
6	8	3	9		9	8	7	
1	5				7	9		

Page 37   It is a pepper mill.

Page 43   Picture 1: Four Mexicans in a revolving door.
Picture 2: A bear climbing up a tree.

Page 45   1. number in the chef's hat
2. bow in apron string
3. stove control at far right
4. Steam in oven
5. Lower right corner of apron

Page 47   He said: "You will hang me." If he is hanged, the statement is true and therefore he must be beheaded. But if he is beheaded, the statement would be false and therefore he must be hanged.

Page 51   Romeo and Juliet are goldfish lying dead on the floor. A gust of wind blew the window open and knocked the fishbowl off the windowsill.

Page 61   It is possible that none of the women fulfill all the conditions.

Page 67   When the people in the church stood up to pray, Charlie the Cockroach crawled onto a pew. When the pastor finished the prayer, the people sat back down…!

Page 77   One of them said: "Hell! I'm a vegetarian…!"

Index